ESSENTIAL CONCEPTS

A COMPLETE GUIDE TO JAZZ THEORY AND IMPROVISATION

**by
Christian Klikovits**

ISBN 0-634-06194-1

7777 W. BLUEMOUND RD. P.O. BOX 13819 MILWAUKEE, WI 53213

In Australia Contact:
Hal Leonard Australia Pty. Ltd.
22 Taunton Drive   P.O. Box 5130
Cheltenham East, 3192   Victoria, Australia
Email: ausadmin@halleonard.com

Visit Hal Leonard Online at
www.halleonard.com

Introduction

The art of jazz piano is a vast subject. A long tradition of talented and dedicated artists have contributed a wealth of beautiful, interesting, and sometimes challenging (in the best sense of the word) music to the genre. The best musicians in this field display astonishing levels of creative invention and technical facility. But jazz music is as much about personal artistic statements as it is about craftsmanship. Among western musical styles, it has the highest percentage of improvisation as opposed to composition. A large part of jazz is the interaction of the musicians with each other, and it is at its best when the players show respect for the legacy of jazz as well as for each other.

Feel is equally important in jazz music. More often than not, jazz is played with a "swing feel." That means that two consecutive eighth notes are not of equal length (as they normally are in classical music); rather, they are played more like the first and third note of an eighth-note triplet. This is just an approximation, though—you can't really notate swing, which is why in notation it is usually written like regular eighth notes. (Instead, there will often be a note at the beginning of the tune to play with a "swing feel.") The only way to really get the feel right is to *listen to the music*. You cannot improvise in a vacuum; in order to play jazz, you have to listen to jazz. Take advantage of the many available recordings of the masters, go listen to live concerts, imitate, emulate, and—most importantly—enjoy yourself.

My goal in this book is to present the reader with a number of important concepts, some of which are specific to jazz music, and others that can be found in other styles as well. It is assumed that you have a basic knowledge of music theory (such as scales, intervals, and chords), and a desire to explore the freedom of improvised music.

The joy of being a good jazz player is well worth the time and effort it takes to become one. I invite you to approach music not only from an artistic, but also from a spiritual perspective; communicating through music is a wonderful way to express who you are as a human being.

About the Audio

The accompanying CD contains audio samples of many of the examples in the book. The 🔊 icon next to the exercise indicates the corresponding CD track number. The final track on the CD is a play-along chord progression with drums and bass only. This progression is used throughout many of the examples in the book.

Piano: Christian Klikovits
Bass: Harald Weinkum
Drums: George Dum

Contents

Part One:
Harmony

Jazz music is harmonically complex. It requires a solid understanding of chord progressions, the harmonic implications of individual chords, and their relation to scales. Chord accompaniment is mostly improvised on the spot. While Western classical music is normally written out, and pop songs mostly require you to play specific parts with little or no room for deviation, jazz pianists often play from *lead sheets*—simple charts with chord symbols that have to be interpreted. Actual notes are usually not written out. The chart might say Dmi7, and it is your job to have a repertoire of voicings available that fit that chord symbol.

This first part of this book introduces the basic harmonic vocabulary of jazz (seventh chords and extended chords), some common chord progressions (such as the II–V–I progression), and a number of ways to translate chord symbols into appropriate voicings.

Seventh Chords

1

The vast majority of jazz literature uses *seventh chords* (and their extensions: ninth, eleventh, and thirteenth chords), rather than the simple triads that make up most pop music and much of the classical repertoire.

Seventh chords are built by adding a 7th interval to a triad. There are five basic seventh chord qualities: major seventh, dominant seventh, minor seventh, minor seventh (flat five), and diminished seventh. Here are all these chords built on C and E.

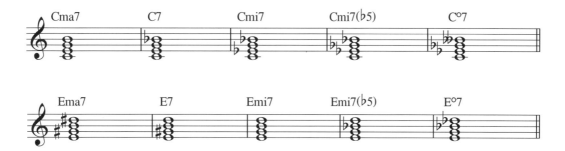

- A *major seventh* chord is a major triad with an added major 7th (a note that is a major 7th from the root of the chord).

- A *dominant seventh* chord is a major triad with a minor 7th added.

- A *minor seventh* chord is a minor triad with a minor 7th added.

- A *minor seventh (flat five)* chord is a diminished triad with a minor 7th added.

- A *diminished seventh* chord is a diminished triad with a diminished 7th added.

Another very important chord is the *minor (major seventh)* chord, consisting of a minor triad and a major 7th.

Two other chords should be mentioned here that are not technically seventh chords, but are used interchangeably with certain seventh chords:

1. The *major sixth* chord (a major triad with a major sixth) is often used instead of a major seventh chord (and vice versa).

2. The *minor sixth* chord is often used instead of a minor (major seventh) chord (and vice versa).

The construction of these eight chord types should be thoroughly understood, and then practiced in all twelve keys. Pay attention to the similarities and the differences between the qualities: lowering the 7th in a major seventh chord, for example, results in a dominant seventh chord; lowering the 5th in a minor seventh chord gives you a minor seventh (flat five) chord; and so on.

Extended Chords

2

Most of the chords in our musical system are built by stacking 3rd intervals on top of each other. A C major triad, for example, consists of the note C, the note E which is a 3rd higher than C, and the note G which is a 3rd higher than E. The seventh chords of Chapter 1 were built by adding another 3rd interval to the top note of a triad. For example, adding the note B (a 3rd up from G) to a C major triad creates a C major seventh chord.

Seventh chords can be further extended by adding additional 3rds on the top. The added notes that are higher than a 7th are called *extensions*, or just *tensions* (which is precisely what these notes are supposed to do: create more tension).

With the exception of diminished seventh chords (which will be discussed in detail later in the book), all the basic seventh chords can be extended with 9ths, 11ths, and 13ths.

Ninth Chords

Ninth chords are created by adding the interval of a 9th above the root (or a 3rd above the 7th) to a seventh chord. Major seventh, minor seventh, and minor seventh (flat five) chords can be extended with a major 9th only. In dominant seventh chords you can use major, minor, or augmented 9ths (though not all at once). There will be more on when to use which in Chapter 9.

Major sixth, minor sixth, and minor (major seventh) chords are also frequently extended with a major 9th.

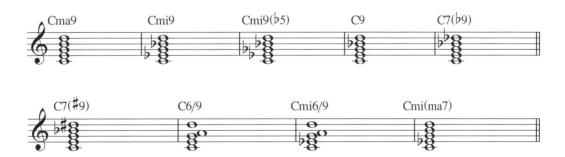

Eleventh Chords

Eleventh chords are created by adding the interval of an 11th above the root (or a 3rd above the 9th) to a seventh chord. Major seventh, major sixth, and dominant seventh chords can be extended with augmented 11ths only, while minor seventh, minor seventh (flat five), minor (major seventh), and minor sixth chords use perfect 11ths.

(For more on why certain chords use augmented 11ths, see Chapter 9.)

When voicing eleventh chords, it is your choice to include the 9th or not (unless it specifically says in the chord symbol to use both 9th and 11th). Most jazz voicings that have an 11th also include the 9th.

Thirteenth Chords

Thirteenth chords are created by adding the interval of a 13th above the root (or a 3rd above the 11th) to a seventh chord. Major seventh and minor seventh chords can be extended with major 13ths only. Minor seventh (flat five) chords can be extended with minor 13ths only. Dominant seventh chords can be extended with either major or minor 13ths (more on when to choose which in Chapter 9). It does not make sense to add a 13th to a major sixth or minor sixth chord, since a 13th is the same note as a 6th, which is already present in the chord.

When voicing thirteenth chords, it is your choice to include a 9th and/or 11th, or not (unless it specifically says in the chord symbol which combination to use).

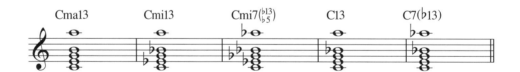

3   II–V–I Progressions

Despite the fact that jazz music is harmonically complex, much of it can be reduced to a single progression, referred to by musicians as *II–V–I* ("two–five–one"). This is the jazz equivalent of the IV–V–I progressions found in classical or pop music. But while a simple pop song might only have the IV–V–I chords of one particular key throughout the whole song, jazz tunes tend to modulate a lot, often using II–V–I progressions in many different keys during one song.

In major keys, the II chord is usually a minor seventh chord, the V chord a dominant, and the I chord a major seventh (or major sixth) chord. In minor keys, the II chord is usually a minor seventh (flat five) chord, the V chord a dominant chord with alterations (see Chapter 9), and the I chord a minor seventh, minor (major seventh), or minor sixth chord. Remember that major seventh and major sixth chords can be used interchangeably, as can minor (major seventh) and minor sixth chords. Often these progressions appear in incomplete form in a song, as in V7–Imi7, or IImi7–V7.

It is very important to recognize these progressions immediately when you encounter them in a chart, or when you hear them being played. For example: Dmi7–G7–Cma7 should automatically register as II–V–I in the key of C major; Bmi7(♭5)–E7 is II–V in the key of A minor (again, the progression does not have to be complete); A♭7–D♭ma7 is V–I in the key of D♭ major.

The figures on the following pages show II–V–I progressions in all major and minor keys, using root-position seventh chords. They should be practiced thoroughly, until each individual progression is ingrained both in the brain and in the hands. I have used root-position voicings to make the chord qualities and and the root movement clearly visible, even though this is not how one would necessarily voice the chords in actual playing.

II–V–I in Major Keys

Track 1

Chapter 3

II–V–I in Minor Keys

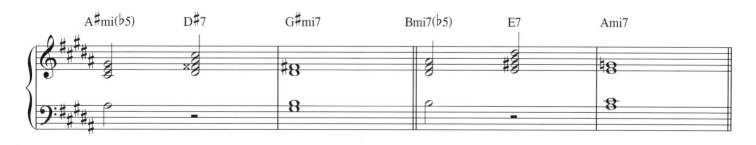

Two-Note Rootless Voicings

4

One of the most important skills of a jazz piano player is voicing chords. The figure below illustrates the difference between a chord (in this case a C major triad) and a *voicing* (one of two many different ways of playing that triad).

Same chord (C major triad), different voicings:

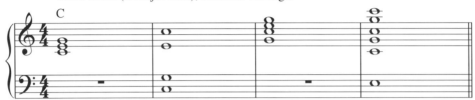

The more complex a chord is, the more different voicings exist for it. The vast majority of jazz music uses a harmonic vocabulary made up of seventh and/or extended chords. How does one approach voicing those chords? In other words, what notes do you play, and in what order? We will start with simple two-note voicings based on the concept of guide tones, and then build from there.

Guide Tones

Guide tones are the two notes that, aside from the root, define the sound of a seventh chord: the 3rd and the 7th (or, in the case of major sixth and minor sixth chords, the 3rd and the 6th).

The following figure shows the guide tones for the first four seventh chord qualities (for diminished chords, refer to Chapter 19). Notice that Cma7 can be voiced with the 3rd and 7th, as well as with the 3rd and 6th.

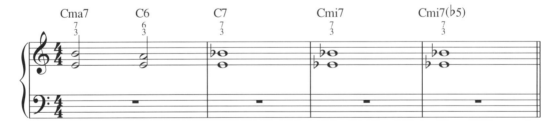

But you might ask, doesn't a chord have to have the root in it? Well, a chord yes, but not necessarily a voicing. In most ensemble situations, you will be playing with a bass player. Usually he or she is the one providing the root of the chord, and you are playing rootless voicings. (Bass players can become rather hostile if you're fiddling around in their territory.)

The simplest rootless voicings are the two-note guide-tone voicings presented here. To hear the full sound of the chord, just add the root in the bass register.

A and B Positions

We will build guide-tone voicings (as well as the three-, four-, and five-note voicings discussed in the next few chapters) from the lowest note up. All of these will have either the 3rd or the 7th (or 6th) as the first, or lowest, note. Therefore they can be categorized into two positions, depending on which note is the lower one.

A-position voicings have the 3rd as the lowest note, and B-position voicings have the 7th as the lowest note.

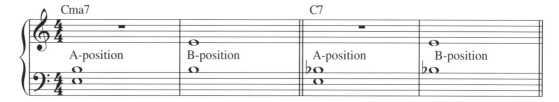

Voice Leading

Voice leading refers to the way in which the notes of a chord move into the next one. It usually sounds best to keep common tones where they are, and move the other notes by as little distance as possible.

Here is this concept in the progression of a C major triad to an F major triad. Example a) demonstrates good voice leading: the common tone C remains where it is, and the other voices move by step. Example b) does not flow very well, and in most situations will sound worse.

The next example shows a IImi7–V7–Ima7 progression voiced with rootless two-note voicings, using smooth voice leading. Notice that the voicings alternate between A- and B-position voicings when moving from IImi7 to V7, and from V7 to Ima7. So if you voice the first chord (the II chord) with an A-position voicing, and you move to the next chord (the V chord) using good voice leading, you'll automatically get a B-position voicing. The next chord (the I chord) then moves back to A position. This is true of all the voicings presented in this chapter and the next, as long as the progression is II–V–I (which, as mentioned before, is by far the most common progression in jazz tunes).

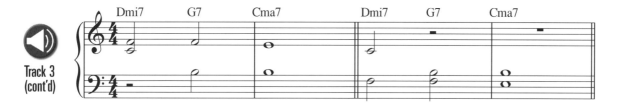

The next four examples illustrate II–V–I progressions in all major and minor keys, voiced with rootless two-note voicings. One should be able to play them with either the right hand (so the left is free to play a bass line) or the left (so the right is free to play melody or solo).

IImi7–V7–Ima7 with two-note voicings: A–B–A

Track 4

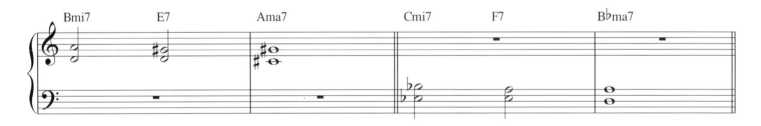

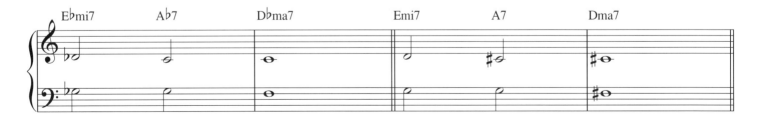

IImi7–V7–Ima7 with two-note voicings: B–A–B

Track 5

IImi7(♭5)–V7–Imi7 with two-note voicings: A–B–A

Track 6

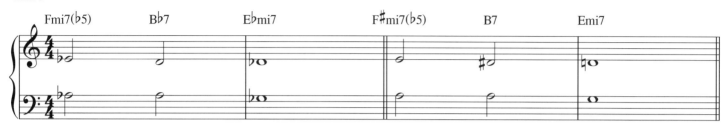

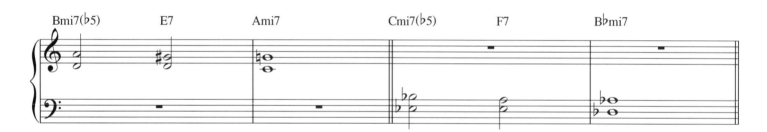

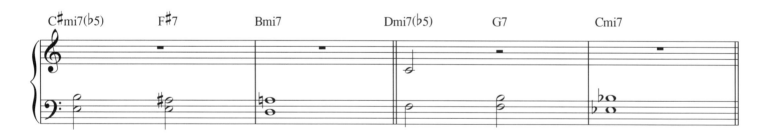

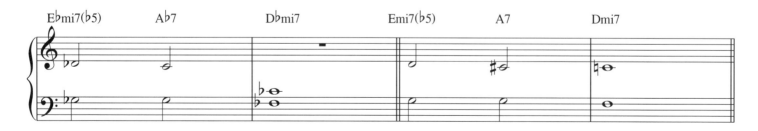

IImi7(♭5)–V7–Imi7 with two-note voicings: B–A–B

Standard Progression with Two-Note Voicings

This example shows two-note rootless voicings being used to voice a thirty-two-measure chord progression typical of standard jazz tunes. It should be played with a swing feel.

5 Three-Note Rootless Voicings

Three-note rootless voicings are created by adding another note on top of the two-note guide-tone voicings of Chapter 4. The extra note will be either a 9th, a 5th, or a 13th.

On major seventh (or major sixth) chords, this results in the following voicings: 3–7–9, 3–6–9, 7–3–5, or 7–3–13.

On minor seventh chords, we'll use ♭3–♭7–9 or ♭7–3–5.

On minor seventh (flat five) chords, we'll use ♭3–♭7–9 or ♭7–3–♭5.

On dominant seventh chords, we'll use 3–♭7–9, 3–♭7–♯9, 3–♭7–♭9, ♭7–3–13, or ♭7–3–♭13.

On minor (major seventh) or minor sixth chords, we'll use ♭3–7–9, ♭3–6–9, 7–♭3–5, or 6–♭3–5.

As with two-note voicings, these three-note voicings are sometimes played with the right hand (with the left hand often playing a bassline) and sometimes with the left hand (with the right playing melody or soloing).

Following are four examples of II–V–I progressions in all major and minor keys, voiced with three-note rootless voicings. To hear the full sound of the chord, just add the root in the bass register.

 ## IImi7–V7–Ima7 with three-note voicings

Track 9

IImi7–V7–Ima7 with three-note voicings: B–A–B

Track 10

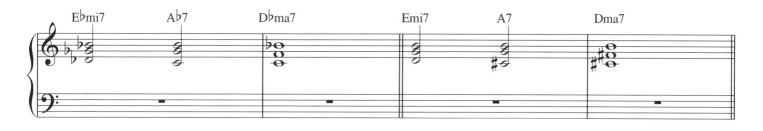

IImi7(♭5)–V7–Imi7 with three-note voicings: A–B–A

Track 11

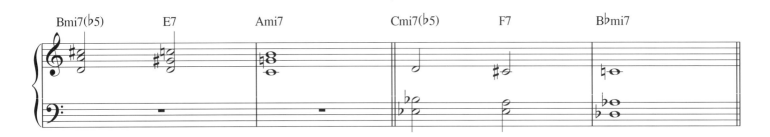

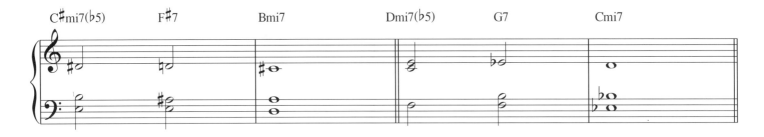

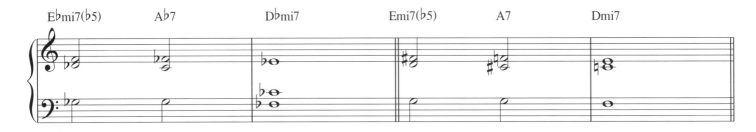

IImi7(♭5)–V7–Imi7 with three-note voicings: B–A–B

Track 12

Standard Progression with Three-Note Voicings

Track 13

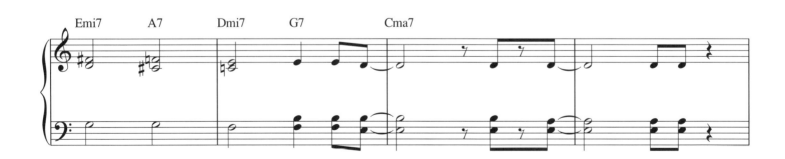

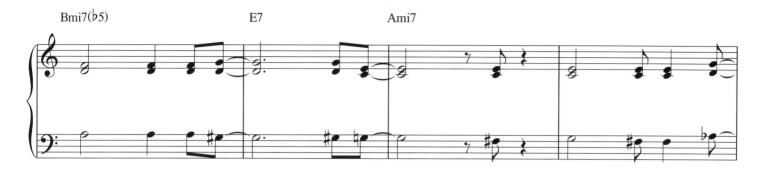

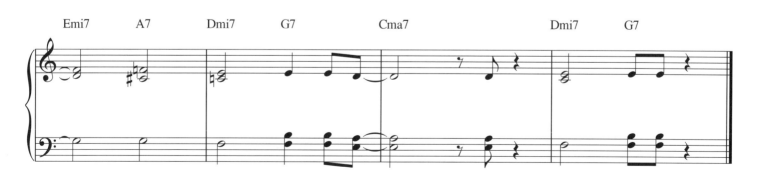

6 Four-Note Rootless Voicings

Four-note rootless voicings come in two types: *close position* and *open position.* In close position, all the notes of the chord are as close together as possible; in all other cases, the chord is in open position.

Close-Position Voicings

These voicings are created by adding an extra note between the lower two voices of the three-note voicings of Chapter 5. The extra note will be either a 9th, a 5th, or a 13th.

On major seventh (or major sixth) chords, we'll use either of the following: 3–5–7–9; 3–5–6–9; 7–9–3–5; 6–9–3–5 or 7–9–3–13.

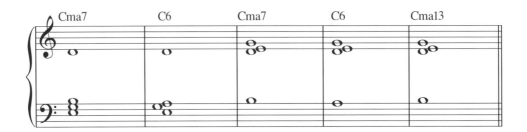

On minor seventh chords, we'll use ♭3–5–♭7–9 or ♭7–9–♭3–5.

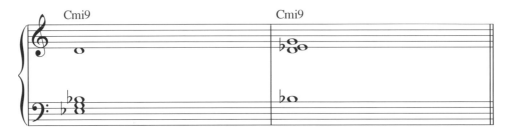

On minor seventh (flat five) chords, we'll use ♭3–♭5–♭7–9 or ♭7–9–♭3–♭5.

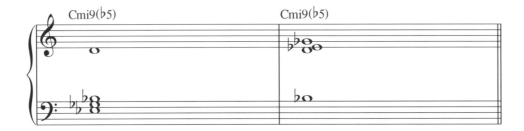

On minor (major seventh) or minor sixth chords, we'll use ♭3–5–7–9; ♭3–5–6–9; 7–9–♭3–5; or 6–9–♭3–5.

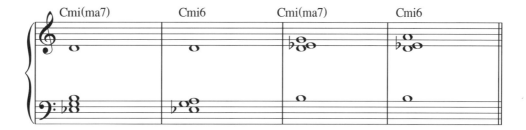

Dominant seventh chords offer the most options, since the 9th and the 13th can both be natural or altered. More often than not, both tensions are either one or the other, but any combination of natural and/or altered 9th and 13th is possible. For now, we'll use the following voicings: 3–13–♭7–9; 3–♭13–♭7–♯9; ♭7–9–3–13; or ♭7–♭9–3–♭13.

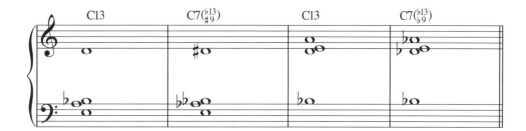

Open-Position Voicings

These voicings are created by adding the same note as in close-position voicings, only an octave higher. For example, an open-position Cma7 voicing would read 3–7–9–5 (compared to 3–5–7–9 in close position). All of the above close-position voicings can be made into open-position voicings by transposing the second note from the bottom up one octave.

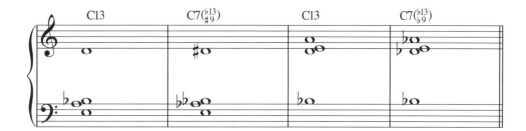

Because these voicings span more than a octave, it is not practical to play them with one hand. Thus, we're entering the realm of *two-handed voicings.* They are used mainly for accompaniment when playing with a rhythm section, but can also be incorporated into solo piano playing.

II–V–I with Four-Note Voicings

The following figures show II–V–I progressions in all major and minor keys, voiced with four-note root-less voicings in open and close positions.

IImi7–V7–Ima7 with four-note voicings (close): A–B–A

Track 14

IImi7–V7–Ima7 with four-note voicings (open): A–B–A

Track 15

6

IImi7–V7–Ima7 with four-note voicings (close): B–A–B

Track 16

IImi7–V7–Ima7 with four-note voicings (open): B–A–B

Track 17

IImi7(♭5)–V7–Imi7 with four-note voicings (close): A–B–A

Track 18

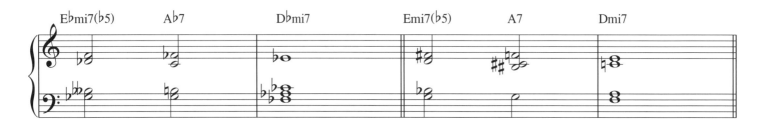

IImi7(♭5)–V7–Imi7 with four-note voicings (open): A–B–A

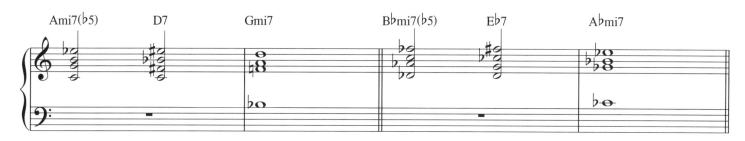

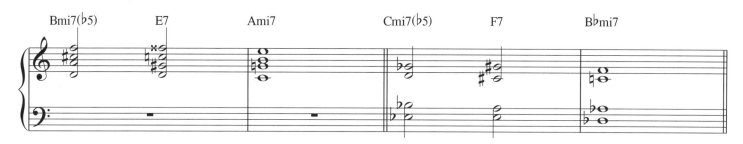

IImi7(♭5)–V7–Imi7 with four-note voicings (close): B–A–B

Track 20

IImi7(♭5)–V7–Imi7 with four-note voicings (open): B–A–B

Track 21

Standard Progression with Four-Note Voicings (Close)

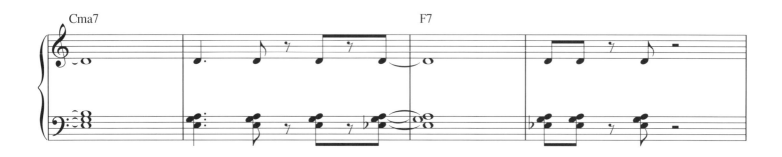

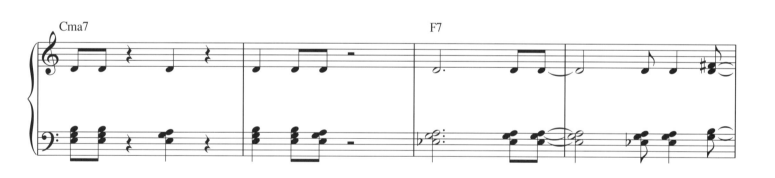

Standard Progression with Four-Note Voicings (Open)

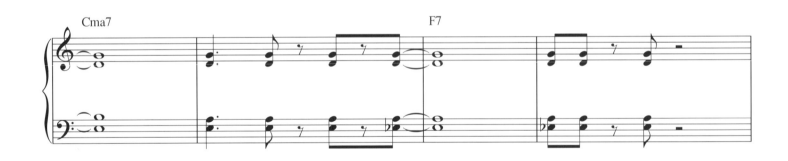

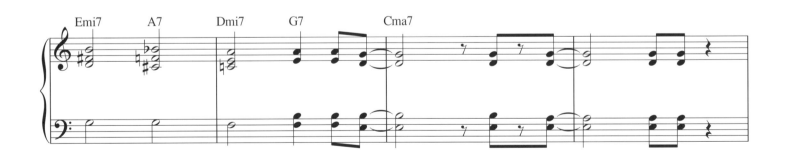

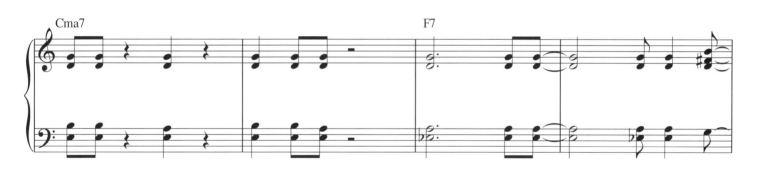

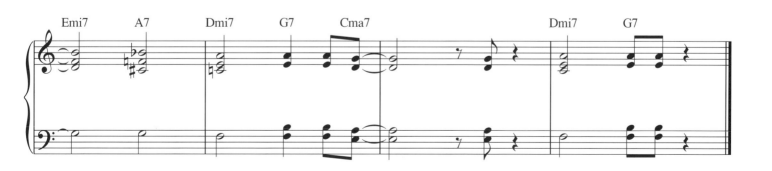

7 Five-Note Rootless Voicings

Five-note rootless voicings are created by adding an extra note on top of open-position four-note voicings. This note can be any chord tone or extension that is appropriate for the chord quality. It usually sounds best if that note is a 3rd, a 4th, or a 5th away from the top note of the four-note voicing. Also, the interval of a minor 9th between any two notes of a voicing should generally be avoided. (We'll explore this further in Chapter 9).

Common Five-Note Voicings

For major seventh or major sixth chords:
3–6–9–5–1; 3–6–9–5–7; 6–9–5–7–3; or 7–3–13–9–5.

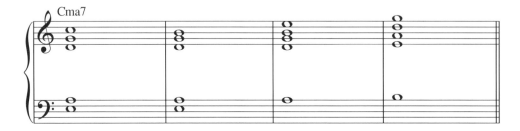

For minor seventh chords:
♭3–♭7–9–5–1 or ♭7–♭3–5–9–11.

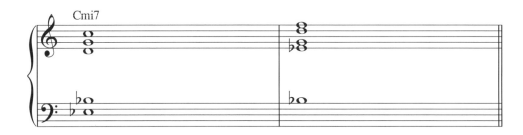

For minor seventh (flat five) chords:
♭3–♭7–9–♭5–1 or ♭7–♭3–♭5–9–11.

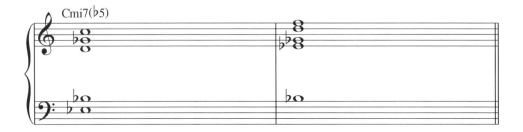

For dominant seventh chords:

3–♭7–9–13–1; 3–♭7–♯9–♭13–♭9; ♭7–3–13–9–5; ♭7–3–♭13–♯9–♯11.

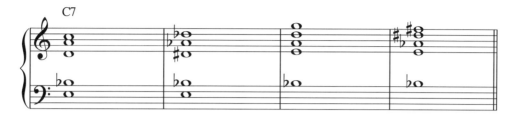

For minor (major seventh) or minor sixth chords:

♭3–6–9–5–7 or 6–♭3–5–9–11.

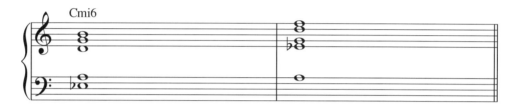

There are many more combinations for five-note voicings, but the ones presented here are a good place to start. Notice that none of the notes in the voicings are doubled.

II–V–I with Five-Note Voicings

Following are II–V–I progressions in all major and minor keys, voiced with five-note rootless voicings.

Track 24

IImi7–V7–Ima7 with five-note voicings: A–B–A

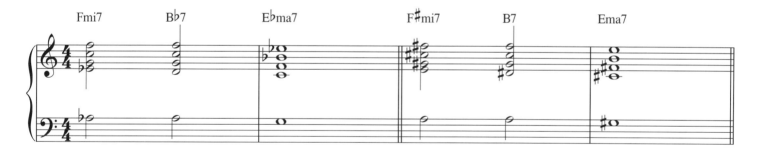

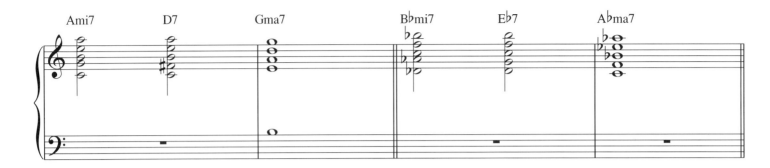

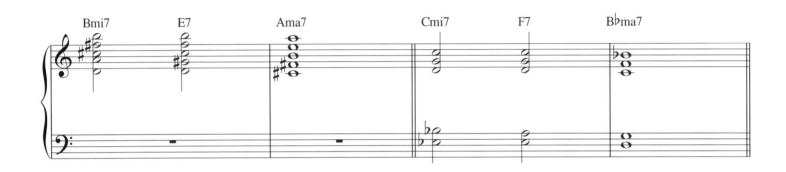

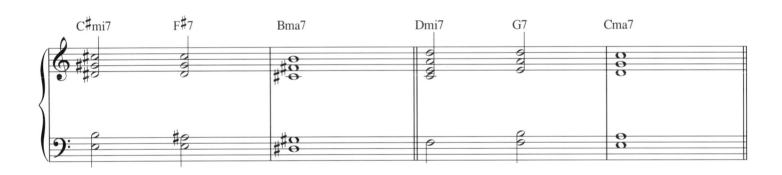

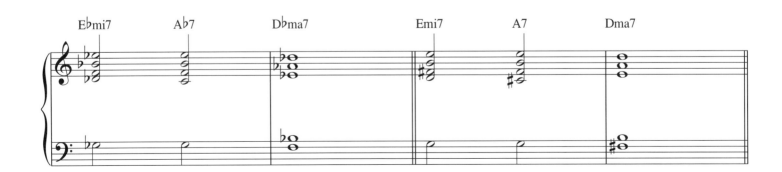

IImi7–V7–Ima7 with five-note voicings: B–A–B

Track 25

IImi7(♭5)–V7–Imi7 with five-note voicings: A–B–A

Track 26

IImi7(♭5)–V7–Imi7 with five-note voicings: B–A–B

Track 27

Standard Progression with Five-Note Voicings

Track 28

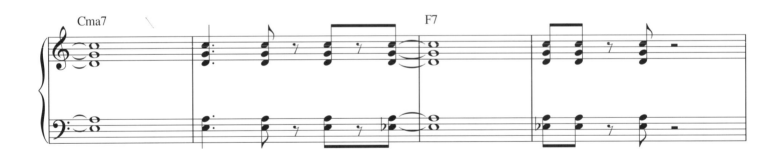

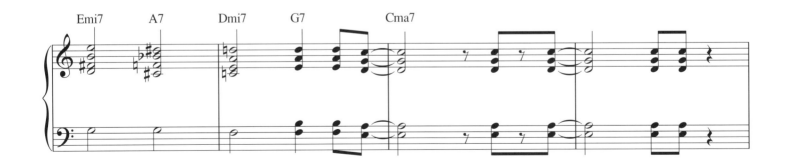

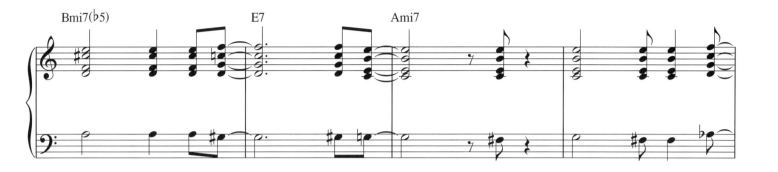

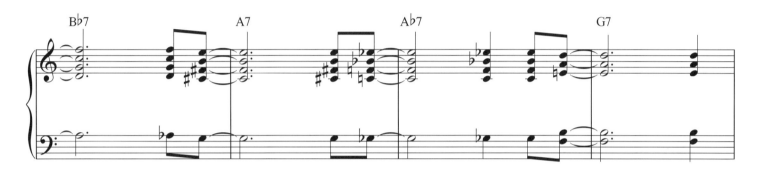

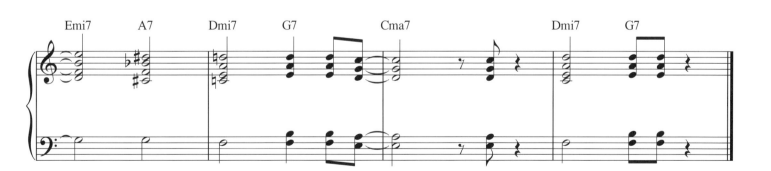

Octave Voicings

8

Octave voicings consist of two separate parts: the left hand playing a three-note or close-position four-note voicing, and the right hand playing 2–4 notes spanning an octave. The left and right hands are usually an octave or two apart.

To find the notes for the right-hand part of octave voicings, follow these steps:

a) Choose a note that fits the chord you're voicing. It can be any note of the scale—9ths, 11ths, 13ths, 5ths, and roots work especially well. (For example, use the 9th of a Cma7 chord, which is the note D.)

b) Playing that note with your thumb, add the same note an octave higher, playing it with your fifth finger.

c) To make the voicing sound fuller, add one or two notes in the middle—perfect 4ths, perfect 5ths, or major 6ths up from the lower note work best. (For example, in that same Cma7 chord, add a G between the two Ds.)

There are many possibilities here; experiment with the concept of octave voicings to find your personal favorites.

These voicings can sound very powerful; they can help the piano player cut through when the band is playing loud, or when the piano is not amplified. They're also very useful for *harmonizing melodies—* just keep the left-hand voicing the same, and play the melody in octaves with your right hand.

II–V–I with Octave Voicings

Following are II–V–I progressions in all major and minor keys, voiced with octave voicings.

 ## IImi7–V7–Ima7 with octave voicings

Track 29

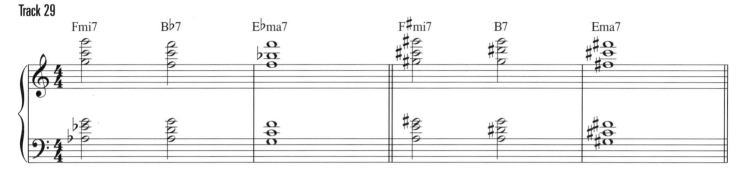

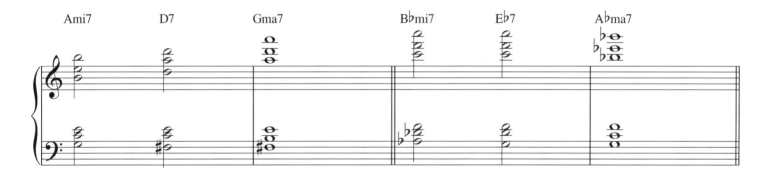

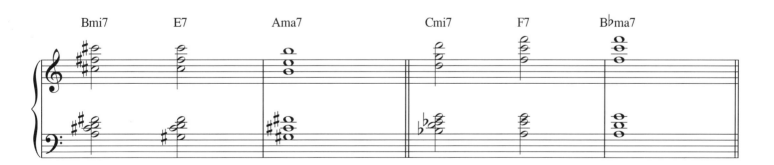

IImi7(♭5)–V7–Imi6 with octave voicings

Track 30

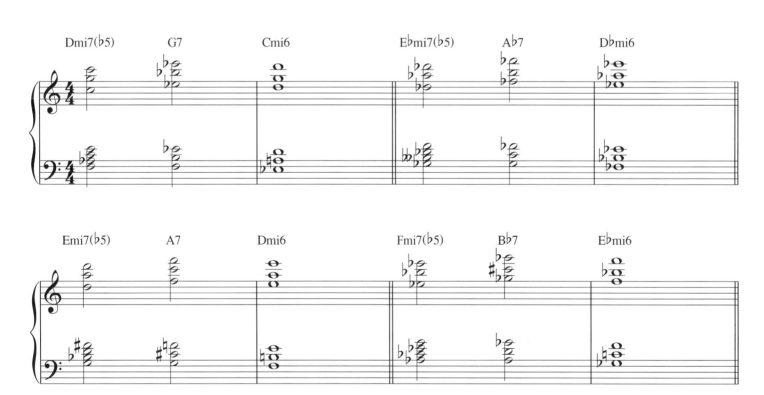

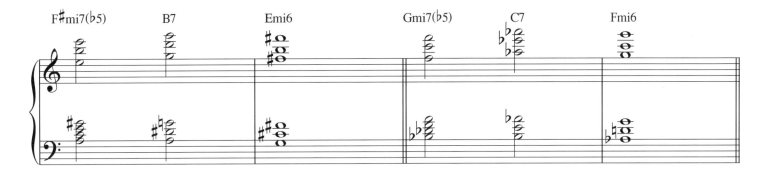

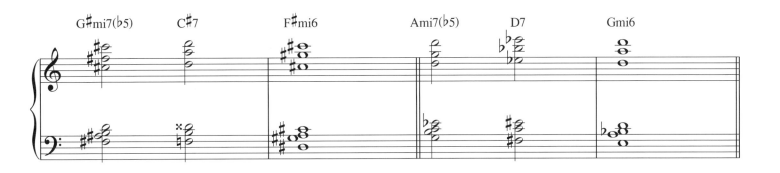

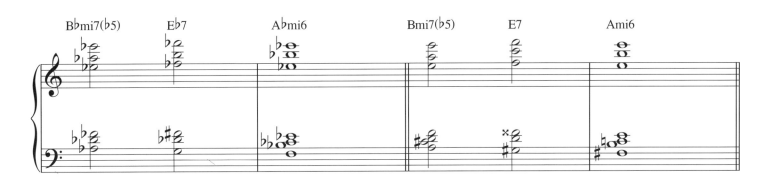

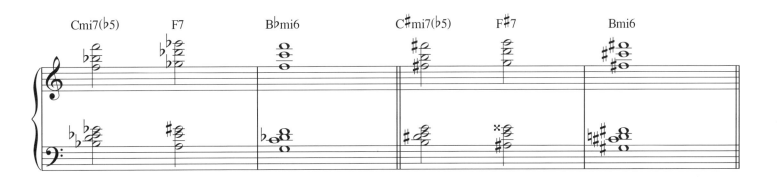

Standard Progression with Octave Voicings

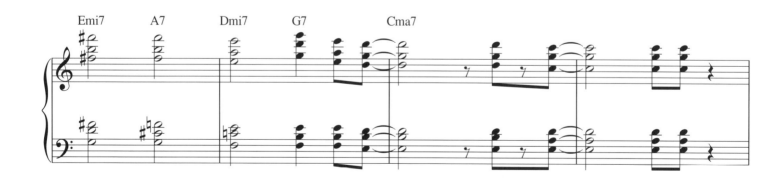

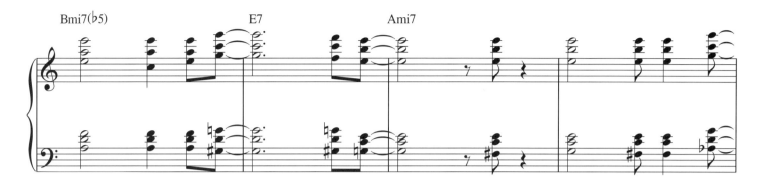

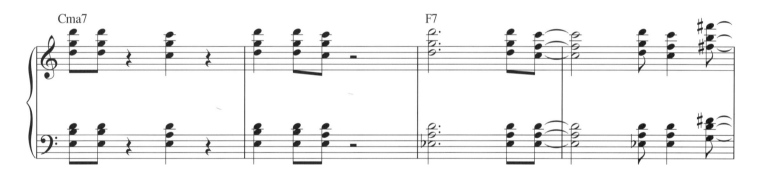

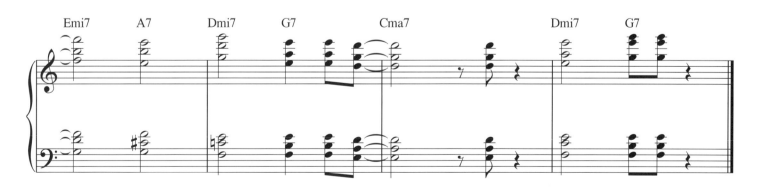

Altered Chords

9

As hinted at in earlier chapters, the chord extensions (9ths, 11ths, and 13ths) can be raised or lowered from their diatonically occurring forms, thus turning into ♭9ths, ♯9ths, ♯11ths, and ♭13ths, respectively. Chords that contain such alterations are called *altered chords*.

Which alterations are possible depends on the quality of the chord:

* Dominant chords are the most frequently altered quality; they can contain every possible alteration (♭9, ♯9, ♯11, ♭13)

* Major seventh chords cannot contain any altered 9ths or 13ths; however, the 11th, if present, is always raised—this is because the natural 11th would create a minor 9th interval with the 3rd of the chord, thereby obscuring the major tonality.

* Minor seventh chords cannot contain any altered extensions.

* Minor seventh (flat five) chords can contain natural 9ths, natural 11ths, and ♭13ths only.

Here are the possible alterations for the various chord qualities.

The reason for altering chords is the same as for adding natural extensions: to add color, dissonance, or character to the chord. Altered notes usually create more tension than natural ones.

So when should you alter chords? As always, the answer to this question depends on many factors such as style, other instruments involved, desired dissonance, and most importantly, personal taste. Basically, any one of the possible alterations can be played at any time. There are, however, certain standards that have evolved over the years. These are not hard-and-fast rules, but merely guidelines that should be used as a starting point for exploration.

The ♯11 in a major seventh chord is a beautiful, but very colorful note that should be used with some restraint. It can stick out and sometimes sound too dissonant. Taste is the key here.

The ♭13 in a minor seventh (flat five) chord is dissonant, but fairly common, and will fit most musical situations.

Dominant seventh chords present the most opportunities for alteration. If the dominant chord resolves to its diatonic major seventh chord (in other words, a perfect 4th up), it can be altered or not. If it resolves to a minor chord a 4th up, it is usually *fully altered* (meaning it contains altered 9ths, and/or 11ths, and/or 13ths). If a dominant chord does not resolve a 4th up, it most commonly contains a natural 9th, and/or a raised 11th, and/or a natural 13th.

Let me emphasize again that these are by no means rules, and they should be ignored frequently in order to find new and interesting ways of musical expression.

The next example demonstrates the use of altered chords in the standard chord progression.

Standard Progression with Alterations

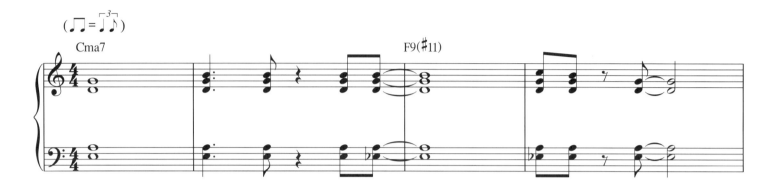

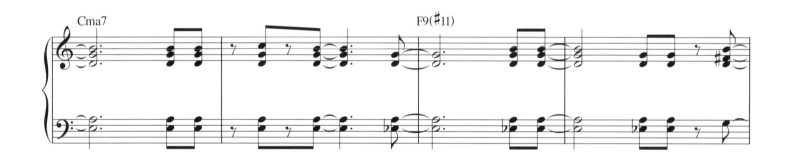

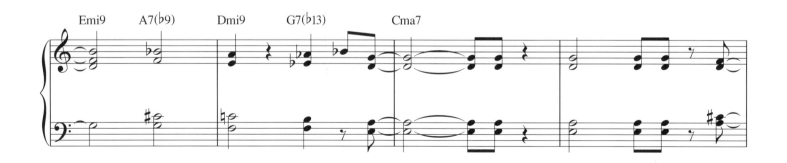

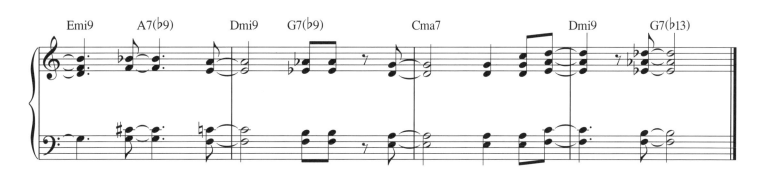

Tritone Substitution

10

Tritone substitution is a very common device in jazz playing. It is based on the fact that two dominant seventh chords that are a *tritone* (or diminished 5th) apart share the same guide tones (introduced in Chapter 4). For example: the 3rd of a G7 chord is B, and the 7th is F; the 3rd of a D♭7 chord is F, and the 7th is C♭ (=B). In other words, two-note rootless voicings for G7 and D♭7 look identical.

Chord substitution in general is used to create variety, to increase the number of colors on our sonic palette. Tritone substitution in particular is commonly used to replace a dominant chord in any given progression. For instance, Dmi7–G7–Cma7 can be changed to Dmi7–D♭7–Cma7, D♭7 being the tritone substitution chord.

Often, a progression will move from the IImi7 chord to the V7 first, and then to ♭II7 (a tritone sub) before resolving to Ima7. In the key of C major, that progression would be Dmi7–G7–D♭7–Cma7.

To extend this concept even farther, a IImi7–V7 can be inserted instead of just a dominant chord. (This is called *functional harmony*; we'll discuss it in Chapter 11). In the key of C major, this would result in Dmi7–A♭mi7–D♭7–Cma7.

Notice that when replacing a dominant chord with its tritone substitution, the resulting chord often looks the same as if you had altered the original dominant chord. In other words, the tritone sub for G7, D♭7, contains the same notes as a fully altered G7 chord—with the exception of the root. This is an example of how musical concepts often overlap, and certain notes or chords can be analyzed in many different ways.

Chapter 10

Track 33

Standard Progression with Tritone Substitutions

This example uses some voicings containing the root of the chord so as to make the substitutions easier to spot.

Functional Harmony

11

Functional harmony is another way to create interest in your comping or harmonizations. Using familiar patterns of tension and resolution (the most common in all Western music being a V chord resolving to I), you can insert chords into otherwise static harmony.

Let's say you have four measures of Cma7, and you want to create more harmonic movement. You could insert a G7 chord anywhere in those four measures, and then return to Cma7.

Track 34

Track 35

Another common possibility is inserting a IImi7 chord before a V7 chord.

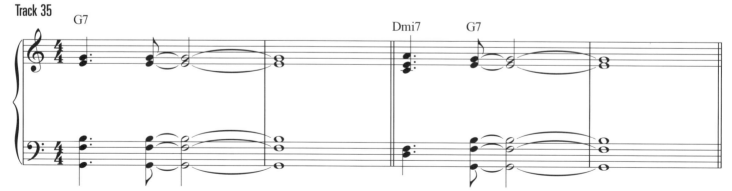

Taking the idea a step further, you could precede your target chord with a V chord, and then precede the V chord with its V chord.

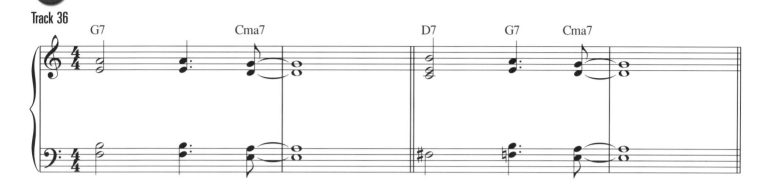

Functional harmony is an excellent tool to use when harmonizing melodies. The following figure shows a simple four-note melody over a Cma7 chord. First it is harmonized using various Cma7 voicings. The second harmonization employs functional harmony, thus increasing the sense of structure and complexity.

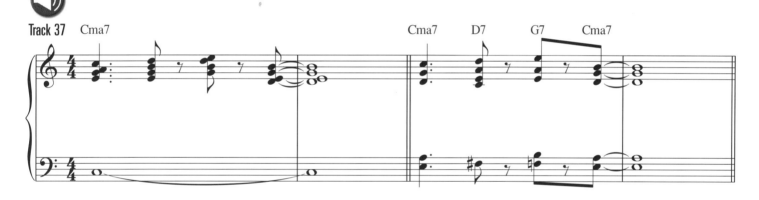

As always in music, the possibilities are endless. Take the basic concept as a starting point and then go where no one has gone before!

Standard Progression with Functional Harmony

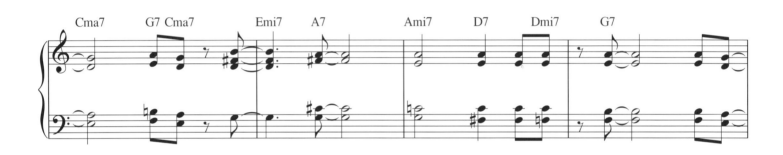

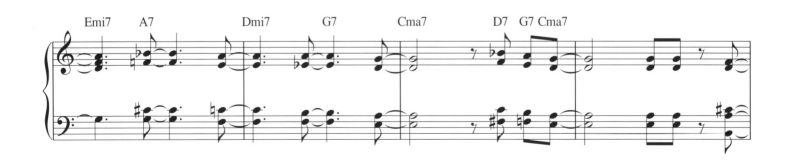

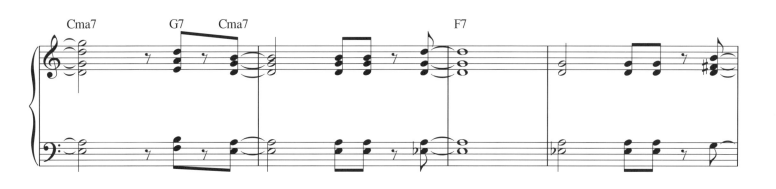

Chromatic Harmony

Chromatic embellishments, both harmonic and melodic, are another very typical sound in jazz music. Chromaticism creates strong temporary dissonance, and is usually resolved by half step. Here are some common techniques using chromaticism.

From the chord you are on, move up or down a half step, and then back.

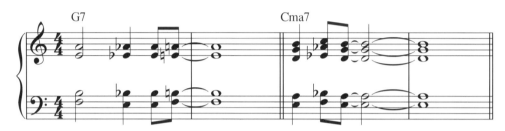

As you move through chords in a progression, insert chromatic steps before resolving to the target chord.

A chord or note can be approached chromatically from both above and below before resolving.

These techniques can be extended to include two chromatic steps in a row.

Note that the chromatic chords are usually of relatively short duration.

Standard Progression with Chromatic Harmony

Track 39

Chapter 12

Part Two: Melody

Improvisation (or spontaneous composition) makes up the biggest part of jazz playing—as opposed to pre-composition, which plays a more important role in many other styles of music. When improvising, most of the time you will be "playing over changes," or improvising chord accompaniment or melodies over a given chord progression.

There are many different approaches when it comes to deciding which notes to play when soloing over changes ("changes" is musicians' shorthand for "chord changes"). This second part of the book will introduce some of the melodic concepts and techniques commonly used by jazz musicians.

Playing over Changes

Usually, the note choices in your solo are determined by two factors:

1) the *quality* of the chord; and

2) its *function* in the progression.

Chord qualities are major seventh, minor seventh, dominant, and so on. The chord names imply different scales or modes that can be used for soloing over them.

Chord function looks at a chord in terms of its relation to the key in which you are playing. For example, a Dmi7 chord in the key of C functions as a IImi7 chord (chord functions are expressed with Roman numerals), because it is built on the second note of the C major scale.

The chord quality usually gives you a number of scale choices, and then the chord function narrows it down to just one or two. In the example cited above, the quality of the Dmi7 chord would fit any number of scales or modes, including natural minor, Dorian, and Phrygian. The chord function, IImi7, tells me that the Dorian mode is the best choice. To find out why, read on...

Scales and Modes

13

There are lots of different scales in Western music—a fact which can be intimidating to the beginning improviser. However, if you look at it the right way, most of it can be reduced to four basic scales. Mastering these scales will enable you to play over almost any chord or chord progression you'll encounter in jazz.

There are four scales every improviser should "speak fluently":

1) the *major scale* and its modes

2) the *melodic minor scale* and some of its modes

3) the *blues scale*

4) the *diminished scale*

The Major Scale

The major scale has been the basis for most of Western music for a long time. Its close relation to the natural overtone series gives it an inherent musical logic that our ears respond to. Chords and melodies derived from the same major scale tend to sound good together.

The figure below shows the twelve major scales for review. The correct fingerings are as follows:

	Fingering	**Key(s)**
Right hand:	1–2–3–1–2–3–4–1(5)	C, D, E, G, A, B
	2–3–1–2–3–4–1–2	D♭
	3–1–2–3–4–1–2–3	E♭
	1–2–3–4–1–2–3–1(5)	F
	2–3–4–1–2–3–1–2	F♯
	3–4–1–2–3–1–2–3	A♭
	4–1–2–3–1–2–3–4	B♭
Left hand:	5(1)–4–3–2–1–3–2–1	C, D, E, F, G, A
	3–2–1–4–3–2–1–3	D♭, E♭, A♭, B♭
	4–3–2–1–3–2–1–4	F♯
	4(1)–3–2–1–4–3–2–1	B

You should be able to play these major scales up and down the keyboard fluently, without much thought about the notes. It needs to be automatic.

The Twelve Major Scales

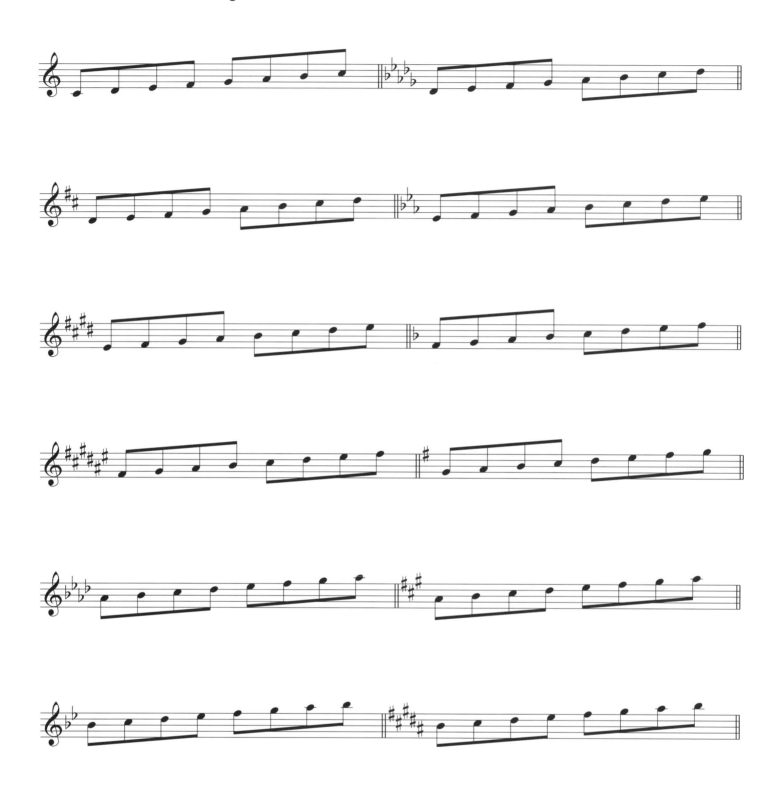

Modes

An important concept relating to scales is that of *modes*. Playing a major scale the regular way, starting on the root, gives you the first mode of the scale. Playing that same scale starting on the second note gives you a different mode. Starting on the third note produces yet another mode, and so on. The concept of modes goes back to Greek antiquity, which is why we still use Greek names for the individual modes of the major scale. There are, naturally, seven of them.

1) The first mode of the major scale is called *Ionian*. It is identical to a regular major scale.

2) The second mode of the major scale is called *Dorian*.

3) The third mode is called *Phrygian*.

4) The fourth mode is called *Lydian*.

5) The fifth mode is called *Mixolydian*.

6) The sixth mode is called *Aeolian* (which is identical to the *natural minor scale*).

7) The seventh mode is called *Locrian*.

Each mode name corresponds to its starting note. Playing a C major scale from C to C is called C Ionian; playing it from D to D is called D Dorian; from E to E is called E Phrygian; and so on. Applying the concept to the key of D major would produce D Ionian, E Dorian, F♯ Phrygian, G Lydian, and so on.

Modes of the C Major Scale

It is important to be able to think of a mode in terms of its parent scale, that is, the scale from which it is derived. C Dorian is a B♭ major scale, played from C as a starting point. G Lydian is a D major scale, played from G.

While all modes of the major scale are useful, some of them are more common than others and therefore more important. The Dorian and Mixolydian modes are ubiquitous, and I will talk about them in more detail in the next chapter. The Lydian mode is the most common scale choice for major seventh chords that don't function as a tonic. The Aeolian mode (better known to many people as the *natural minor scale*) is used frequently with minor-key chord progressions.

Again, the important thing to remember is that all these modes are just variations on one single "parent scale." Learning to improvise using one major scale automatically puts seven scales at your disposal, and enables you to play over several different chord types. In the next chapters I'll talk more about the practical application of scales and modes.

Originally, modes were only derived from the major scale. However, there are other scales that can be used in the same way—most notably the melodic minor scale.

The Melodic Minor Scale

After the major scale, the *melodic minor* scale is the most useful scale for jazz improvisation. The harmonic language of jazz is full of complex, colorful chords, which call for equally colorful scales. The beautiful, rich sound of melodic minor is perfectly suited to accommodate a lot of those chords. Melodic minor can be thought of as a major scale with a lowered 3rd, or as a minor scale with a major 6th and a major 7th scale degree.

The following figure shows all twelve melodic minor scales. The correct fingerings are as follows:

	Fingering	**Key(s)**
Right hand:	1–2–3–1–2–3–4–1(5)	C, D, E, G, A, B
	1–2–3–4–1–2–3–1(4)	F
	4–1–2–3–1–2–3–4	B♭
	3–1–2–3–4–1–2–3	E♭
	3–4–1–2–3–1–2–3	A♭
	2–3–1–2–3–4–1–2	D♭, F♯
Left hand:	5(1)–4–3–2–1–3–2–1	C, D, E, F, G, A
	3–2–1–4–3–2–1–3	D♭, A♭
	4–3–2–1–3–2–1–4	F♯
	4(1)–3–2–1–4–3–2–1	B
	2–1–4–3–2–1–3–2	B♭, E♭

With the exception of the right hand in F♯, and the left hand in B♭ and E♭, all the melodic minor scale fingerings are the same as the ones for the major scales.

The Twelve Melodic Minor Scales

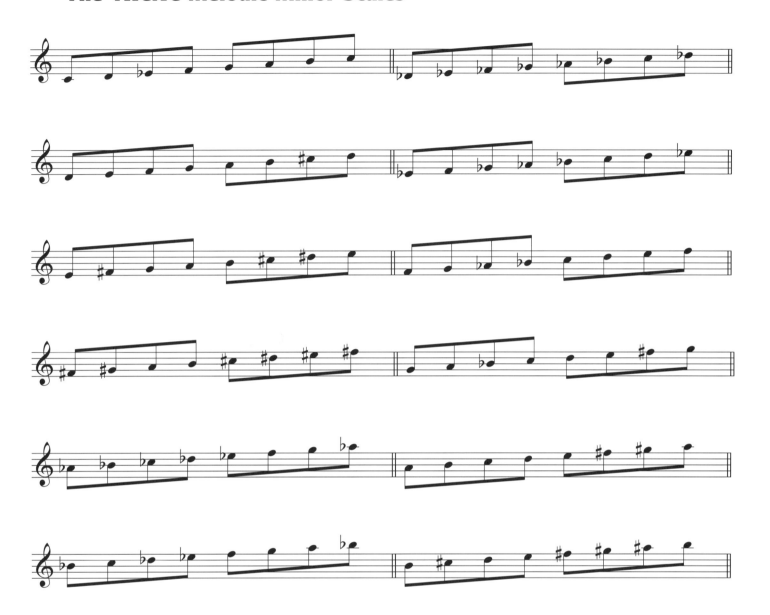

Modes of the Melodic Minor Scale

As with major scales, modes can be derived from the melodic minor scale. However, only four of the seven modes are commonly used.

1) The first mode of melodic minor (the regular *melodic minor scale*) is used to play over minor chords that function as a tonic: minor sixth and minor (major seventh) chords.

2) The fourth mode of melodic minor is called *Lydian ♭7* (pronounced "Lydian flat seven"). It is used over dominant chords with natural 9th, natural 13th, and raised 11th.

3) The sixth mode of melodic minor is called *Locrian ♮2* (pronounced "Locrian sharp two"). It is played over minor seventh (flat five) chords with a natural 9th.

4) The seventh mode of melodic minor is called the *altered scale*. It is played over dominant chords with altered 9th, 11th, and/or 13th.

The following figure shows the most commonly used modes of the C melodic minor scale. Playing the scale from C to C is called C melodic minor. Playing the scale from F to F is called F Lydian ♭7. Playing the scale from A to A is called A Locrian ♯2. Playing the scale from B to B is called B altered.

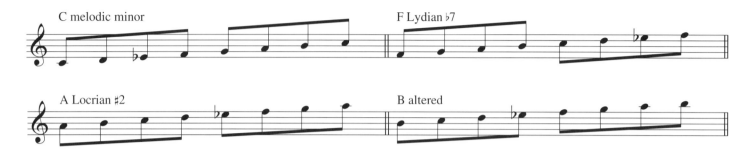

It follows that any melody derived from the C melodic minor scale will sound good on a number of chords: Cmi6, Cmi(ma7), F9(♯11), Ami7(♭5), and B7alt. Here is an example of this:

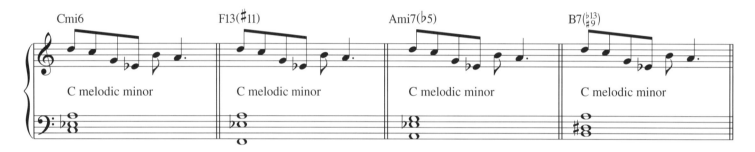

Looking at it from the perspective of the individual chords, we see that over a minor sixth or minor (major seventh) chord we can play the melodic minor scale starting on the root of the chord—that one is pretty obvious. Over a dominant chord with 9, and/or 13, and/or ♯11, we can play the melodic minor scale starting a perfect 5th above the root. Over a minor seventh (flat five) chord, we can play a melodic minor scale starting a minor 3rd above the root. Over a dominant chord with ♭9/♯9, and/or ♯11, and/or ♭13, we can play a melodic minor scale a half step up from the root.

The following example demonstrates the use of melodic minor scales over these four chord qualities. Over Cmi6 I used the C melodic minor scale; over C9(♯11) I used the G melodic minor scale; over Cmi7(♭5) I used the E♭ melodic minor scale; and over C7(♭9) I used the D♭ melodic minor scale.

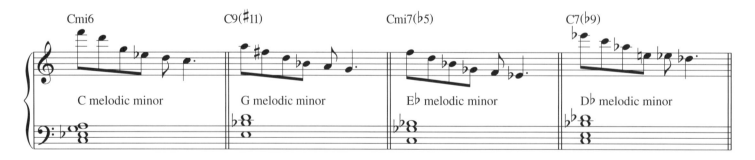

This juxtaposition of a chord and a scale that have different roots creates interest in and of itself, and also makes it easier to come up with colorful melodies that one wouldn't necessarily think of otherwise. Thorough knowledge of the melodic minor scale is imperative in jazz improvisation. We will see a lot more of this scale in the following chapters.

The Blues Scale

The blues, in addition to being an important genre in its own right, has influenced virtually every type of popular music in the last fifty years. It is also an integral part of the jazz language. Certain elements of the blues (such as the use of the blues scale, the use of the dominant chord as a tonic, and the twelve-bar blues form) are very common in jazz. But while blues players use these devices almost exclusively, jazz players use them as part of their arsenal, alternating and combining them with many other elements. It is easy to overuse the blues sound in a jazz standard; as always in music, tastefulness is the key.

The figure below shows the blues scale in all twelve keys. It should be practiced with both hands, spanning several octaves. There are no official fingerings for the blues scale (there isn't even an official blues scale, but the one shown here is agreed upon by most musicians), but here are suggested fingerings:

	Fingering	**Keys**
Right hand:	1–2–3–4–1–2–1(3)	C, D, E, G, A
	1–2–3–1–2–3–1(4)	D♭, E♭, F, F♯, A♭, B♭, B
Left hand:	3–2–1–3–2–1–3	D, E♭, E, F♯, G, A, B♭, B
	5(1)–4–3–2–1–2–1	C, F
	2–1–2–1–4–3–2	D♭, A♭

The Blues Scale in All Twelve Keys

II–V–I Progressions
14 And What to Play over Them

As mentioned earlier, II–V–I is the most common chord progression in jazz music. To improvise successfully, you need to be able to spot these progressions immediately, and interpret them in terms of appropriate scale choices.

To reiterate: the following root movements constitute II–V–I progressions. Note that some of the notes may be spelled enharmonically; for example, the progression E♭mi7–A♭7–D♭ma7 can also appear as D♯mi7–G♯7–C♯ma7.

D–G–C	E♭–A♭–D♭	E–A–D
F–B♭–E♭	F♯–B–E	G–C–F
A♭–D♭–G♭	A–D–G	B♭–E♭–A♭
B–E–A	C–F–B♭	C♯–F♯–B

Each of the chords can have several qualities.

II chord: minor seventh, minor seventh (flat five)

V chord: dominant

I chord: major seventh, major sixth, minor sixth, minor (major seventh), minor seventh, dominant

Any combination of these chord qualities is possible within the II–V–I progression, but the following are by far the most common:

- **II–V–I in major keys:**   IImi7–V7–Ima7 or I6

- **II–V–I in minor keys:**   IImi7(♭5)–V7–Imi6 or Imi(ma7)

                                IImi7(♭5)–V7–Imi7

- **II–V–I in blues:**   IImi7–V7–I7

74

II–V–I in Major Keys

Key Center

Let's look at a II–V–I progression in the key of C major: Dmi7–G7–Cma7. Dmi7 is a diatonic chord in the key of C major, built on the second note of the scale. G7 is the diatonic chord on the fifth degree of the scale. Cma7, obviously, is the tonic chord. Since all three chords are *diatonic* (meaning they only use notes of the C major scale), it follows that the C major scale can be played over the whole progression. This is the simplest way to approach soloing over chords, and it is called the *key center* approach. You take a number of chords belonging to the same major or minor tonality, lump them together, and use a single scale to improvise over them. The advantage is that you don't have to think about switching scales, and can concentrate on building good melodies instead (which, after all, is the point of playing a solo).

Track 40

The figure below shows the use of the major scale over several IImi7–V7–Ima7 progressions.

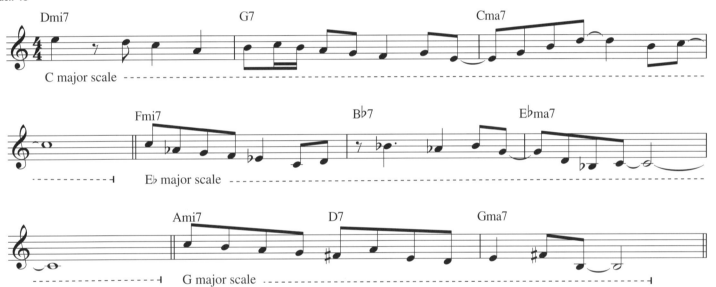

Chord/Scale

Another approach to soloing is called the *chord/scale* approach. In this case, you look at each chord individually, and choose an appropriate scale. This is more complex and therefore more challenging. The advantage is that it can yield more interesting, colorful melodies, and it also helps you deal with progressions that are beyond the scope of the key center approach.

Looking at the above progression from the chord/scale point of view, we first have the Dmi7 chord. The best scale choice is Dorian (you can hardly go wrong with Dorian on minor seventh chords—it is by far the most common choice). On the Cma7 chord, we'll use the C major scale (which is the logical choice for tonic major seventh chords).

The G7 chord, however, presents a number of different possibilities. If we choose Mixolydian, then we have D Dorian on the Dmi7 chord, G Mixolydian on the G7 chord, and the C major scale on the Cma7 chord. All three scales are modes of the C major scale, so we might as well go back to the key center way of thinking and play C major over the whole progression—which is cool. However, another option would be to choose a different scale for the G7—and that is *way* cool. The most common alternate scale choice for a V7 chord in a major key is the altered scale. We've seen that altered is the seventh mode of melodic minor, so over G7 we can play Ab melodic minor. The whole progression then would read: D Dorian—A♭ melodic minor—C major. Here are several examples of this.

Track 41

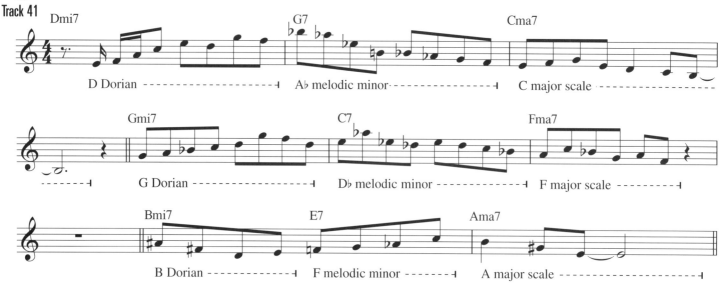

To sum up, for a IImi7–V7–Ima7 progression, try one of these two approaches: play the major scale of the Ima7 chord over the whole thing (the key center approach), or play Dorian on the minor seventh chord, melodic minor a half step up on the seventh chord, and the major scale on the major seventh chord (the chord/scale approach). There are many other combinations and scale choices, but these two are the most common, and they will almost always work well.

II–V–I in Minor Keys

Key Center

Let's look at the following chord progression: Dmi7(♭5)–G7alt–Cmi7. As with the major keys above, there are two ways of approaching this progression. From a key center perspective, we find that all three chords are diatonic in C minor, and therefore we can play a C natural minor scale over all of them. You will hear a lot more dissonance in this case than in a major-key II–V–I, and you have to be somewhat more discriminating in your note choices. However, the principle is the same: three chords and one scale; focus on creating good melodies. (Technically, the G7 chord is derived from C harmonic minor, but for the purpose of key center this can be ignored—just use C natural minor.) Here's an example of the key center approach over Dmi7(♭5)–G7alt–Cmi7.

Track 42

Chord/Scale

For the chord/scale approach, try this: on the Dmi7(♭5) chord, use F melodic minor. (Remember that on minor seventh (flat five) chords, a very good scale choice is melodic minor starting on the minor 3rd.) On the G7alt chord, use A♭ melodic minor. (Altered dominant chords use the melodic minor scale a half step up.) On the Cmi7 chord, use C Dorian or C natural minor. Next is an example.

Track 43

The I chord in minor progressions is often a minor sixth or minor (major seventh) chord. This enhances the tonic sound of the chord, as in Dmi7(♭5)–G7alt–Cmi6. On the Cmi6 chord, the best scale choice is C melodic minor.

Track 44

The Blues Scale over II–V–I

In blues, the I chord is usually a dominant seventh chord. Jazz players will often give a bluesy flavor to tunes that are not technically blues by turning Ima7 or I6 chords into I7 chords. Sometimes this is done flat out, and sometimes it is more implied. Below is a II–V–I progression in the key of C major—first using the C major scale, and then implying a dominant quality by using the C blues scale

Track 45

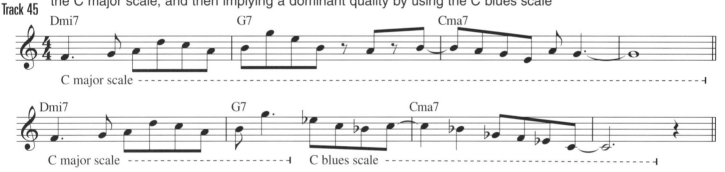

The key center approach is ubiquitous in blues. In fact, much of the characteristic sound of the blues comes from the use of a single scale (the blues scale) over whole progressions, or even entire tunes.

On dominant chords with a tonic function (or over IImi7–V7–I7 progressions) you can use the blues scale built on the root of the key, or the blues scale built on the major 6th of the key. Here's a Dmi7–G7–C7 progression, first with the C blues scale, and then with the A blues scale.

Track 46

As mentioned before, there are lots of different variations on the II–V–I theme. The ones discussed above are the most common, but by no means the only ones. However, they are a good starting point, and once you get a feel for it you'll be able to explore it in a less categorized and more creative way.

Minor Chords

15 And What to Play over Them

So far we've looked at minor chords in the context of II–V–I progressions. If they function as IImi7 chords, the Dorian mode is always a safe bet. If they have tonic function, as in IImi7(♭5)–V7–Imi7, both Dorian and the natural minor scale work well. On minor sixth chords with tonic function, melodic minor works best.

These approaches account for most of the minor chords you'll encounter. Here are a few examples of the exceptions—minor chords functioning as something other than IImi7, Imi7, or Imi6.

IIImi7

The IIImi7 chord is frequently used as a substitute for Ima7. In the progression Emi7–Ami7–Dmi7–G7, the Emi7 chord substitutes for Cma7.

All of the chords are diatonic in the key of C major, so the C major scale would work well over the whole progression. On Emi7, that results in an E Phrygian mode (Phrygian being the third mode of the major scale, and E being the third note of the C major scale), but I prefer to think C major over all the chords—it's just easier.

Track 47

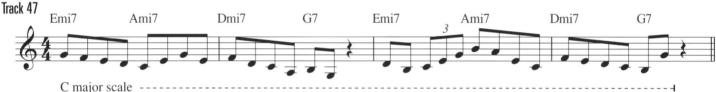

Another common progression in the key of C major is Emi7–A7–Dmi7–G7. You could treat Emi7 the same way as above and just play C major over it, or you could look at Emi7–A7 as IImi7–V7 in the key of D major, and play the D major scale over both chords (in which case, you would once again be playing Dorian over the minor seventh chord).

Track 48

Chapter 15

VImi7

Just like IIImi7, the VImi7 chord often appears in diatonic progressions in a major key, as in the afore-mentioned Emi7–Ami7–Dmi7–G7. The C major scale is a good choice on the Ami7. Here it gets a little ambiguous, because of the relation between C major and A minor; they are relative keys, meaning they share the same key signature, and hence the same basic scale (C major and A natural minor contain the same notes). In the above example, there is no reason to think of the Ami7 chord as anything other than a diatonic VImi7 chord in the key of C major, so we play a C major scale over it.

However, in many cases the VImi7 chord adopts more of a tonic function (usually when preceded by its V7 or IImi7(♭5)–V7). In that case, one could argue that the tune modulates back and forth between relative major and minor keys, and treat the minor seventh chord as Imi7. If you then play natural minor over it, you're playing the relative major scale, anyway. Or you could play Dorian, which gives the minor seventh chord a little more distinction from the major key center.

Songs frequently mix relative major and minor keys; their close relation makes them sound good together, while at the same time providing harmonic interest.

Another common occurrence is the VImi7 chord as part of a IImi7–V7 progression. In the key of C major, this would be Ami7–D7, which can be treated like any other IImi7–V7.

The following figure shows several examples involving VImi7 chords.

Track 49

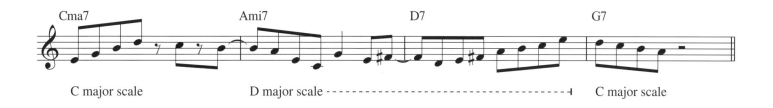

IVmi7

The IVmi7 chord is diatonic in minor keys, and Dorian mode is the best scale choice. It also occurs in major keys, often as part of a turnaround, as in Cma7–Fmi7–Cma7, and again, Dorian is the way to go.

Track 50

IVmi6 or IVmi(ma7)

In major keys, you'll frequently find a IVmi6 or IVmi(maj7) chord, in the same context as IVmi7. The scale of choice, as almost always on these chords, is melodic minor.

Track 51

Sometimes you'll encounter minor seventh chords outside of a diatonic context. A lot of more contemporary tunes feature chords that don't have traditional diatonic relationships (they're often called *modal* tunes or progressions). Dorian is usually a safe choice, even though other minor scales can work as well.

In practical application, music is more ambiguous than it's made out to be (for educational purposes) here: concepts overlap; solos jump back and forth between different scales on the same chord, there's chromaticism, and so forth. Anything you read in this book should be taken as a starting point for your own exploration. The final judge of what sounds good and what doesn't is always your own ear.

16 Major Seventh Chords
And What to Play over Them

As mentioned before, this book uses major seventh and major sixth chords interchangeably, so everything you read about major seventh chords in this chapter also goes for major sixth chords.

If a major seventh chord functions as a tonic (which they very often do), the major scale is the appropriate choice. If a major seventh chord is not the tonic of the key, and it is not preceded by its dominant chord, then the Lydian mode (the fourth mode of the major scale) works best.

If a major seventh chord is not the tonic of the key, but it is preceded by its dominant chord, then both the major scale and the Lydian mode can work. (The preceding dominant chord can make the major seventh chord sound more like a tonic; that's why the regular major scale often works in this case.)

Track 52

Here are many major seventh chords and scales in action.

Dominant Chords
17 And What to Play over Them

As in traditional Western music, the dominant chord in jazz music is the most colorful one—the point in a progression with the most tension. Even though the rules of resolution are much more liberal in jazz than in other styles, the basic arc of tension and release also applies to jazz. Dominant scales therefore provide a lot more color and dissonance than scales for other chord types.

Dominant chords appear as non-diatonic chords more often than other chord qualities. Here are a few basic rules that will work most of the time:

1) If the dominant chord resolves to a major chord a perfect 4th up (as in G7–Cma7), use either Mixolydian, or altered (see also Chapter 14 on II–V–I progressions).

2) If the dominant chord resolves to a minor chord a perfect 4th up (as in G7–Cmi7), use the altered scale (see also Chapter 14 on II–V–I progressions).

3) If the dominant chord does not resolve a perfect 4th up (as in G7 to anything other than a C chord), and it is not the diatonic dominant (V) chord of the key you're in, use Lydian ♭7 (the fourth mode of melodic minor). If it is the diatonic dominant chord of the key you're in, play Mixolydian (if you're in a major key) or altered (if you're in a minor key).

Non-diatonic dominant seventh chords can appear on almost any scale step of any given key. Some of the more common ones are ♭II7, II7, ♭V7, ♭VI7 and ♭VII7. Lydian ♭7 is the best scale choice on all of them.

Track 53

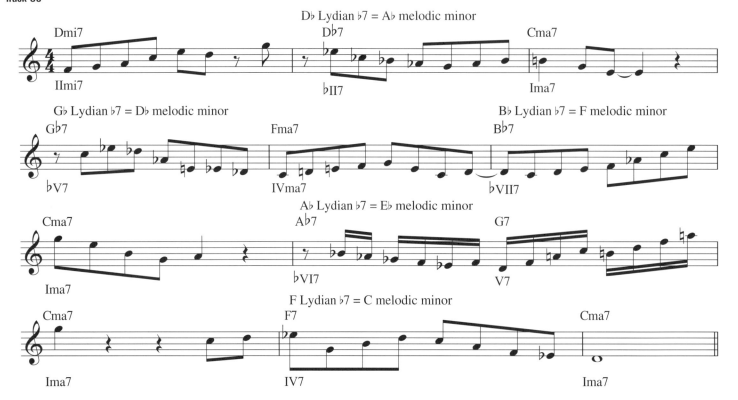

82

Chapter 17

Dominant Chords with Tonic Function

If the dominant chord functions as a I chord—as in most blues tunes—the Mixolydian mode and the blues scale (on the root, or on the 6th) works best. Alterations are used to increase the feeling of tension and resolution in progressions, but since a tonic dominant chord IS the resolution, one won't usually use altered scales over them.

Here are a few examples of melodies over tonic dominant chords.

18 Minor Seventh (Flat Five) Chords
And What to Play over Them

Minor seventh (flat five) chords almost always appear as part of a IImi7(♭5)–V7 or IImi7(♭5)–V7–Imi7 (or Imi6) progression. There are two possible scale choices: the Locrian mode (the seventh mode of the major scale), and Locrian ♯2 (the sixth mode of the melodic minor scale). The regular Locrian mode has a minor second, while Locrian ♯2, as the name implies, has a major second.

Both scales are played frequently, and both are colorful scales (just as minor seventh (flat five) chords are very colorful, with a strong tendency towards resolution). Locrian is the more diatonic-sounding choice, while Locrian ♯2 is more dissonant because of its characteristic major second interval—most lines using Locrian ♯2 emphasize that note.

Track 55

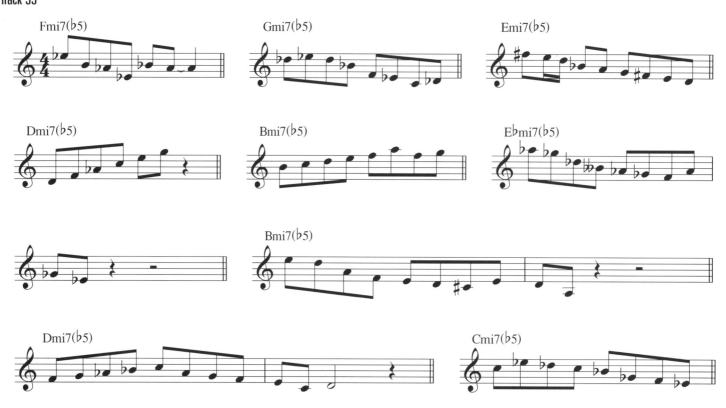

84

Diminished Seventh Chords
19 And the Diminished Scale

Diminished seventh chords have a very unstable sound and a strong tendency towards resolution. The scale associated with diminished harmony is called the *diminished scale*. It is a symmetrical scale that alternates between whole steps and half steps. Here is a C diminished scale.

Because of the symmetrical nature of the scale, everything in diminished harmony and melody can be repeated in minor third intervals; there are really only three diminished chords and scales. The following figure shows diminished scales built on C, C♯, and D. The diminished scale built on E♭ contains exactly the same notes as the C diminished scale (enharmonic notes notwithstanding); the same is true for diminished scales built on G♭ and A.

The next figure shows a C°7 chord and an E♭°7 chord. They contain the same notes—the E♭°7 chord can be looked at as an inversion of C°7.

Note that often diminished scales or chords from the same group don't look exactly alike because of different enharmonic spellings, but they still sound alike.

The three diminished scales are as follows:

1) **C** diminished scale (same as **E♭**, **G♭**, and **A** diminished scales)

2) **C♯** diminished scale (same as **E**, **G**, and **B♭** diminished scales)

3) **D** diminished scale (same as **F**, **A♭**, and **B** diminished scales)

The same is true for diminished seventh chords:

1) **C°7** (same as **E♭°7**, **G♭°7**, and **A°7**)

2) **C♯°7** (same as **E°7**, **G°7**, and **B♭°7**)

3) **D°7** (same as **F°7**, **A♭°7**, and **B°7**)

Diminished Scales and Chords

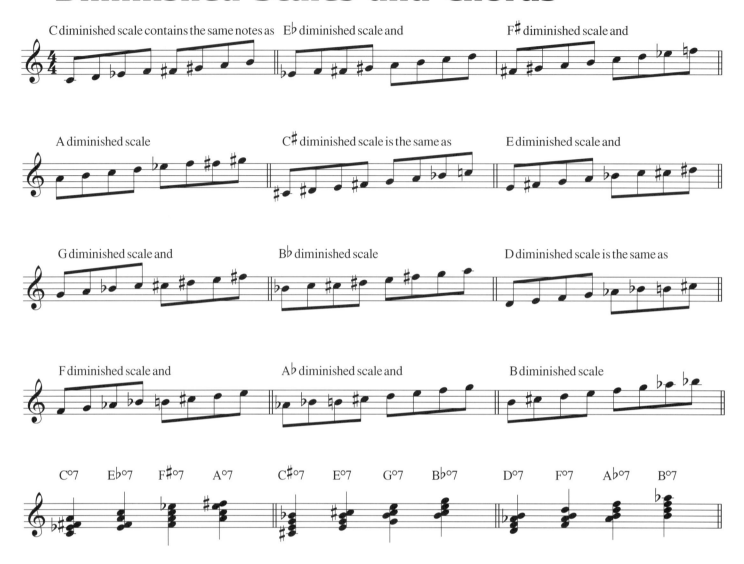

Diminished scales sound very unusual and colorful, partly because they're not derived from any diatonic major or minor context. Melodies can easily sound mechanical because of the symmetry inherent in the scale.

Two Tetrachords

To familiarize yourself with the sound and feel of the diminished scale, try breaking it up into two *tetrachords* (groups of four notes) starting on the root and the diminished 5th. Notice that each individual tetrachord looks like the first four notes of a minor scale.

first four notes of C minor - - - - - - - - - - - ┤   first four notes of F# minor - - - - - - - - - ┤

Chapter 19

Melodic Techniques

The diminished seventh chord consists of consecutive minor 3rds. When soloing over this chord, jazz players often use arpeggios of that basic chord, or the other three in that family (remember, everything repeats in minor 3rds)—here are a few examples of this.

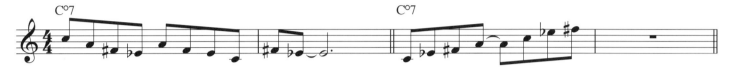

To break up the symmetry a little, raise the top note a whole step, as shown below—this works for both chords and melodies.

Another common melodic device is approaching chord tones by a whole step from above and a half step from below before landing on the target note.

The next figure shows a number of common voicings for diminished seventh chords. Again, keep in mind that moving these chord structures around in minor 3rds gives you more voicings from the same diminished family. Example b) shows one voicing repeated in minor 3rd intervals; c) and e) employ common melodic embellishments in the top voice of the chord.

Diminished Seventh Progressions

In the context of chord progressions, diminished seventh chords usually fall into one of three categories:

1) If the diminished seventh chord resolves up a half step to the root of the following chord, it functions as a VII°7 chord; usually this is a substitute for a V7(♭9) chord

2) Sometimes the duration of a tonic chord is interrupted by a diminished seventh chord on the same root to create harmonic motion within the context of static harmony, as in Cma7–C°7–Cma7.

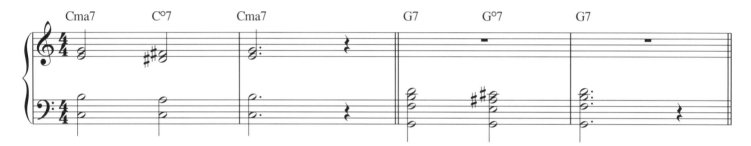

3) Chromatic passing chords: diminished seventh chords are frequently used to chromatically connect two chords whose bass notes are a whole step apart. Here are several examples.

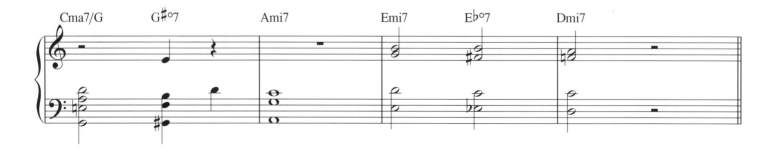

Building Melodies

20

Once you've determined which scale you want to use for improvisation, your task is to build melodies using the available notes, without just running up and down the scale (which tends not to sound very interesting). Our ears respond to certain concepts such as structure, symmetry, and repetition, but also to surprise, variety, and tension and release.

A soloist aims to find a good balance between the expected and the unexpected. Of course, there are many opinions about where exactly that balance lies—which is a good thing; otherwise everybody would sound the same. As always, the ultimate authority is your own ear. However, by listening to and analyzing solos, you'll find that there are certain devices all jazz musicians use, simply because they sound good. Following are a number of suggestions for building coherent melodies.

Scale Patterns

This refers to the practice of playing a scale in symmetrical patterns, as opposed to just playing it up and down like you do in beginning piano lessons. As with all the techniques that follow, you will want to refrain from overusing it; jazz musicians might just go through a pattern once or twice at any given time, then move on to a different idea.

Here are a few scale patterns.

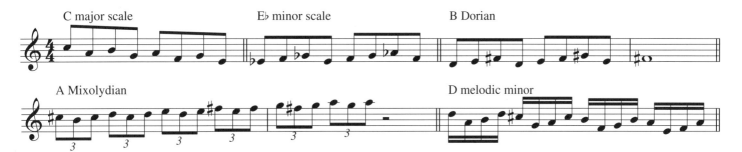

Arpeggios

One of the most common ways of organizing melody notes, an *arpeggio* is a chord played one note at a time. Very often, arpeggios outline the quality of the chord, as in the melody notes C–E–G–B played over a C major seventh chord.

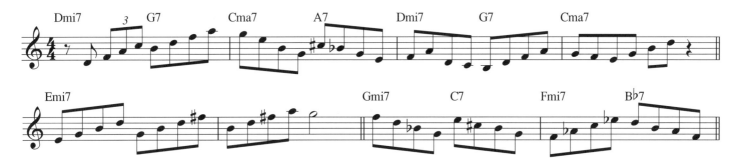

Digital Patterns

Digital patterns are small groups of notes from a scale (often four notes) that are played as a unit. They can be described as scale degrees, such as 1–2–3–5, 3–5–6–7, 1–3–5–3, etc.

Here are a few melodies built on digital patterns.

Chromatic Passing Notes

Chromaticism is used very frequently in jazz solos to break up the predictability of purely diatonic melodies, and to provide color and dissonance. There are no hard and fast rules for using chromatic notes, but some of the more common occurrences are:

- a chromatic passing note between 5 and 6 in major scales

- a chromatic passing note between 8 and ♭7 in dominant scales

- a chromatic passing note between 4 and ♭3 in minor scales

- two chromatic passing notes between 3 and 5 in major or dominant scales

Below are some examples of chromatic passing notes.

Chromatic Approach Notes

Chord tones are often approached by half step (usually from below); sometimes it is in the form of grace notes. The following example illustrates the use of *chromatic approach* notes.

Chapter 20

Enclosure

Often a target note (consonant to the chord you're on) is approached first from a step above, and then from a step below. This is called *enclosure* (or surrounding tones, or changing tones). Both approach notes can be diatonic or chromatic, and both can be a half step or a whole step from the target note. Here are some examples.

Targeting the 3rd

Next to the root, the 3rd is the note that most defines the quality of a chord. Improvisers take advantage of this by frequently targeting the 3rd right at the transition from one chord to the next.

This list is by no means complete. Extensive listening to—and transcribing of—solos will reveal many more ways in which jazz players spontaneously create melodies that make musical sense.

A Standard Solo

Throughout this book, I have tried to present concepts in isolation, so as to make them easier to comprehend. An example of using the major scale over a II–V–I progression featured only the major scale; in two measures illustrating arpeggios, I used arpeggios exclusively; and so on. In real life, of course, things are not as clear-cut. Concepts overlap—improvisers may use several techniques in one measure. There's "outside playing" (temporarily leaving and then returning to a proper scale for the chord you're on), and all manner of wonderful musical messiness that defies our analytical minds.

This final chapter contains a sample solo chorus over the chord progression introduced in the first part of the book. In it, all the soloing concepts introduced in Part 2 are put to work. This should be of some help in understanding how to use the concepts introduced throughout the book. Following are some suggestions as to how to look at the note choices.

The key is C major, so on the tonic Cma7 chord in measures 1 and 2 the C major scale is an obvious choice. The notes used on the first six beats spell out an E minor pentatonic scale (a minor pentatonic scale starting on the 3rd sounds very good on major seventh chords); then there's a diatonic enclosure in the middle of measure 2: D and B resolving to the target note C. The last four notes in measure 2 form an arpeggio, an inversion of the basic C major seventh chord.

The F7 chord in measures 3 and 4 is IV7—a dominant chord that does not resolve to its I chord. As usual, Lydian ♭7 is the best scale choice, and F Lydian ♭7 is the fourth mode of C melodic minor. There's only one note that's different from the C major scale, and that's the 3rd, E♭. That note is emphasized in measure 3, and in bar 4 it is the last note before the harmony changes back to Cma7. There I play E natural, thereby reinforcing the transition from C melodic minor to the C major scale.

Measure 6 features a VI7 chord, and I've used the A altered scale, which is the seventh mode of B♭ melodic minor. The G♯ at the end of the measure is a chromatic passing note, connecting the G before it to the A on the first beat of the next measure.

The next chord is D7, which is II7 in the key of C. Lydian ♭7 is the most appropriate scale choice here. D Lydian ♭7 is derived from A melodic minor, so it is not surprising that the melody notes spell out an Ami(ma7) arpeggio. The notes B and G♯ at the end of the measure form an enclosure resolving to the target note, A.

The G7 in measure 8 is the diatonic V7 chord, leading back to Cma7. I use the digital pattern 9–7–6–5 derived from G Mixolydian (identical to the C major scale) in the first half of the measure, and then change to G altered (= A♭ melodic minor) in the second half of the measure, increasing the dissonance right before the resolution to the Cma7 chord. The notes there spell out an A♭mi(ma7) arpeggio.

Measure 9 shows a chromatic passing note between the 5th and 6th scale degrees on a major seventh chord. On the F7 chord in measures 11 and 12, the scale again is C melodic minor. Notice the enclosure in the middle of measure 11 (F and D resolving to E♭), and the E♭ma7(♯5) arpeggio (E♭–G–B–D) at the end of that measure. E♭ma7(♯5) is the III chord of the harmonized C melodic minor scale. You can try the arpeggios of all the chords derived from the melodic minor scale you are using.

Measures 13 and 14 contain a IIImi7–VI7–IImi7–V7 progression in the key of C major. Emi7–A7 is a diatonic IImi7–V7 progression in the key of D major, so I use the D major scale over both chords. In measure 14 I use the C major scale, except for the last note, Ab. Instead of the diatonic note A, which is the natural 9th in a G7 chord, I use the b9, Ab. Once again, this increases the tension right before resolving back to Cma7. Notice that I target the 3rd of the chord on A7, Dmi7, and G7. Also, Emi7, Dmi7, and G7 all feature arpeggios.

Measure 15 moves back to the C major scale. In measure 16, starting on beat 3, I'm already using the D melodic minor scale, thereby anticipating the next chord, Bmi7(b5), by half a measure. This is common, and it helps move things along by creating a sense of urgency, especially at the transition between different sections of the tune.

In the next few measures, the song modulates to its relative key, A minor. For the Bmi7(b5) chord in measure 17, I've chosen D melodic minor (= B Locrian ♯2). Again, the maj7(♯5) arpeggio found on the 3rd degree of the melodic minor scale is used. Since the E7 chord in measure 18 resolves a 4th up to a minor chord, I used E altered (= F melodic minor), this time using the Dmi7(b5) arpeggio found on step 6 of the F melodic minor scale, followed by an inverted Abma7(♯5) arpeggio starting on beat 3. In measures 19 and 20, I use Ami6 to reinforce the tonic function of the chord. The scale of choice is A melodic minor. Notice the chromatic enclosure Bb–G♯–A in the middle of measure 19.

Starting in measure 21, a series of chromatic dominant chords brings us back to the key of C major. F melodic minor is used on the Bb7 chord, E melodic minor on A7, and Eb melodic minor on Ab7—all of which are Lydian b7 scales of the respective chords. On the G7 chord, using the G altered scale (= Ab melodic minor) gets us back to Cma7. The phrase in measure 24 is one of the all-time most common jazz licks. It is well worth practicing in every key.

There's an enclosure at the beginning of measure 25: F♯–A–G. The chromatic line at the end of measure 26 evokes the sound of the blues. Measure 27 features the familiar C melodic minor scale on F7. In measure 28 there's a chromatic passing note between G and A.

Measures 29 and 30 feature a IIImi7–VI7–IImi7–V7 progression in the key of C. I'm thinking key center and using the A blues scale (which works very well in the context of a blues in C) over both measures. This creates a lot of dissonance between the melody notes and the chords, but the overall sense of tonality and the familiar sound of the blues make it work. Notice that even though the chord symbol in measure 30 says Dmi7, I play D7, using chord substitution to add forward momentum.

At the end of the solo I switch to two-handed voicings—this is a good way to tell the listener and your fellow musicians that you're finishing your solo.

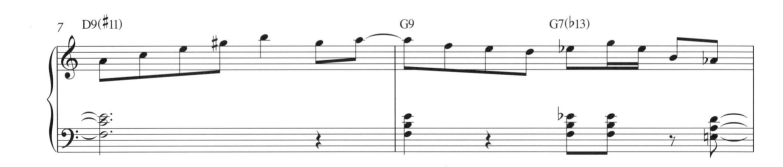

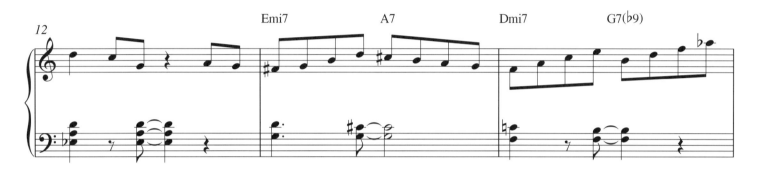

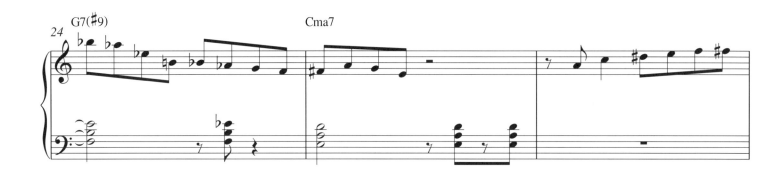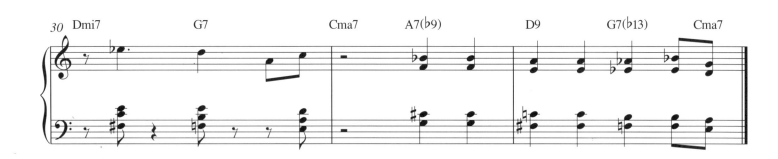